RACE IN
AMERICA

D1278013

RACE IN THE
CRIMINAL JUSTICE SYSTEM

BY ALEXIS BURLING

CONTENT CONSULTANT
Toya Like, PhD
Associate Professor of Criminal Justice & Criminology
University of Missouri–Kansas City

Essential Library

An Imprint of Abdo Publishing | abdopublishing.com

ABDOPUBLISHING.COM

Published by Abdo Publishing, a division of ABDO, PO Box 398166, Minneapolis, Minnesota 55439. Copyright © 2018 by Abdo Consulting Group, Inc. International copyrights reserved in all countries. No part of this book may be reproduced in any form without written permission from the publisher. Essential Library™ is a trademark and logo of Abdo Publishing.

Printed in the United States of America, North Mankato, Minnesota
042017
092017

THIS BOOK CONTAINS
RECYCLED MATERIALS

Interior Photos: Brett Coomer/Houston Chronicle/AP Images, 5; Texas Department of Public Safety/AP Images, 7; Andy Alfaro/ Texas Department of Public Safety/AP Images, 10; David J. Phillip/ AP Images, 12–13; Detroit Publishing Company/Library of Congress, 16–17; Hubbard & Mix/Library of Congress, 20; National Photo Company Collection/Library of Congress, 23; AP Images, 26; iStockphoto, 28–29, 52–53, 64–65, 74–75, 88–89; Shepard Sherbell/ Corbis Historical/Getty Images, 31; Michael Schwartz/New York Post Archives/(c) NYP Holdings Inc/Getty Images, 33; Mel Evans/AP Images, 38–39; Paul Sakuma/AP Images, 40; Red Line Editorial, 44; Guillermo Arias/AP Images, 45; Ross D. Franklin/AP Images, 48–49; Joseph Sohm/Shutterstock Images, 56; Erik McGregor/Pacific Press/ Sipa/AP Images, 59; Eric Risberg/AP Images, 60–61; LM Otero/AP Images, 68; Pat Sullivan/AP Images, 70; Brian Bohannon/AP Images, 72; Rogelio V. Solis/AP Images, 80; Evan Vucci/AP Images, 83; Melanie Stetson Freeman/The Christian Science Monitor/AP Images, 85, 97; Melanie Stetson Freeman/Christian Science Monitor/Getty Images, 86; Emily Rose Bennett/The Grand Rapids/AP Images, 91; Patrick Semansky/AP Images, 93; Rich Pedroncelli/AP Images, 98

Editor: Nick Rebman
Series Designer: Maggie Villaume

PUBLISHER'S CATALOGING-IN-PUBLICATION DATA

Names: Burling, Alexis, author.
Title: Race in the criminal justice system / by Alexis Burling.
Description: Minneapolis, MN : Abdo Publishing, 2018. | Series: Race in America |
    Includes bibliographical references and index.
Identifiers: LCCN 2016962260 | ISBN 9781532110368 (lib. bdg.) |
    ISBN 9781680788211 (ebook)
Subjects: LCSH: Discrimination in criminal justice system--Juvenile
    literature. | --Race discrimination--Juvenile literature. |
    Minorities--Juvenile literature.
Classification: DDC 364--dc23
LC record available at http://lccn.loc.gov/2016962260

CONTENTS

CHAPTER ONE

THE DEATH OF SANDRA BLAND

Twenty-eight-year-old Sandra Bland was feeling refreshingly optimistic on the afternoon of July 10, 2015. *Sandy Speaks*, her video blog about the economic constraints facing her fellow African Americans, was starting to attract followers. After several difficult months of being out of work and without health insurance, Bland had also found a temporary job at her alma mater, Prairie View A&M University. Two days earlier, she had driven 16 hours straight for the interview, from Chicago, Illinois, to Prairie View, Texas.

The position would last only four weeks. And the pay, at $13.80 per hour, wasn't great. Taking the job also meant saying good-bye to her family and relocating to Texas. Still, Bland was intrigued by the university's offer to pay for a master's degree in political science. She jumped at the opportunity and accepted on the spot.

Uplifted by her decision, she stopped by the university's financial aid office to share the good news with an old friend who worked there. They talked for nearly an hour. "She was a fireball, and I was a fireball," said Kyal Webster. "We had a few heart-to-hearts about what it meant to act as a professional. She was ecstatic."[1]

Bland's upbeat mood didn't last long. After she left Webster's office, she was pulled over for what would normally be a routine traffic stop—failing to signal during a lane change. But what happened next was far from routine. According to dashboard camera footage released in the days following the event, Texas state trooper Brian Encinia—a 30-year-old white male—threatened Bland with a Taser and demanded that she get out of the car. After Bland did so, Encinia handcuffed her and forced her to the ground.

When backup arrived, Bland was taken to Waller County Jail. For two days, family and friends promised they would raise the money for her bail. Their efforts were in vain. At 9:00 a.m. on July 13, Bland was found

Footage from the squad car shows Encinia arresting Bland.

unconscious in her cell. According to the coroner's report, she had committed suicide by creating a noose out of a garbage bag.

ANSWERS UNKNOWN

In the weeks and months that followed, people across the country were desperate for answers to explain what might have happened in the days leading up to Bland's death. A reporter from *Chicago* magazine wrote in a December 2015 profile of Bland, "How could someone who was so ecstatic about starting a new job, who was so passionate about the Black Lives Matter movement and had every incentive to share her own experience, who, just hours earlier, seemed primed for a legal battle— how could this person so quickly reach such depths of despair?"[2]

People close to Bland insisted the person they loved couldn't have taken her own life. Some friends believed she was targeted by Encinia because of the color of her skin. Bland's four sisters said although she had endured a few run-ins with the law in the past—driving while intoxicated, drug possession charges, and a few traffic tickets for which she served time in jail—the idea that she would kill herself over an arrest was preposterous. Their mother agreed. "I'm the mama," Geneva Reed-Veal said at her daughter's funeral. "And I'm telling you that my baby did not take herself out."[4]

But another story began to emerge after the district attorney in Waller County, Texas, alerted

A ROUTINE TRAFFIC STOP OR RACIAL PROFILING?

When Encinia saw Bland's car on the afternoon of July 10, 2015, he made a U-turn and began following her. She maneuvered into the right lane to let him pass. Instead, he pulled her over.

Was this a case of racial profiling? Maybe not. But according to *Chicago* magazine, it isn't the first time race has played a factor in Prairie View politics. In 2004, the year before Bland arrived at the predominantly black university, the city's district attorney threatened to arrest any student who tried to vote in local elections—despite a Supreme Court ruling granting students the right to do so.

In 2007, Glenn Smith, the police chief of the nearby city of Hempstead, was accused of acting violently and exhibiting racist tendencies while on patrol. He was suspended for two weeks without pay. A year later, he was elected sheriff of Waller County, the position that oversaw the jail where Bland died. He insists race was not a factor in her death. On November 9, 2016, Smith was reelected, receiving 65 percent of the vote.[5]

Critics of the Waller County Jail said Bland did not receive the psychiatric services she needed.

the Federal Bureau of Investigation (FBI) and opened an investigation into Bland's death. An intake form from the jail where Bland was being held indicated she had tried to kill herself once before, after a complicated pregnancy in which she lost the baby. Because of this red flag, jail regulations specified that Bland should have been seen by

a mental-health professional or put on suicide watch. This
didn't happen.

Instead, Bland was locked up in a cell by herself
for long stretches of time. When neighboring inmates
reported hearing uncontrollable sobs coming from her
cell on Sunday, none of the guards went to check on the
situation. Then on Monday, just before 8:00 a.m., Bland
used the emergencies-only intercom. She begged for more
free calls to her family instead of having to use the phone
inside her cell, which cost $14.99 per call. Her repeated
requests were denied. Less than an hour later, Bland
was dead.

MINORITIES TREATED UNFAIRLY?

In the year following the Sandra Bland case, more than
815 people died in the United States while in jail,
according to a study published in the *Huffington Post*.
Some of these inmates had not been convicted of a crime
and were in custody for less than 21 days. Many were
African American. "Black people are more likely to die in
jail because they are more likely to be arrested than any
other racial group, for reasons that have as much to do
with double standards in the justice system and historic
oppression as they do with crime," the article stated.[6]

Sandra Bland's mother speaks with reporters following her daughter's death.

According to the US Department of Justice, there were an average of 981 inmate deaths per year in US jails and prisons between 2000 and 2013. (Jails are typically used for short sentences, while prisons are used for long

sentences.) The lowest count occurred in 2011, when 525 white people died compared to 234 black people. The highest tally occurred in 2007, when 548 white people died compared to 398 black people.[7]

What do these figures mean? Is the US criminal justice system stacked against African Americans as the article in the *Huffington Post* suggests? Or do the numbers—at least in US jails—tell another story? What about other minorities, such as Hispanic Americans or immigrants? Do white people enjoy a privilege that other races do not?

Throughout US history, race has played a role in the way people have been treated in all aspects of society. This has been the case from the days before the American Civil War (1861–1865), when many African Americans were enslaved, to today. Race was a defining factor in the way politicians and law enforcement handled the war on drugs during the 1980s and 1990s. And it has continued to influence the way Americans think about immigration over the past decades. There are also inequities within the criminal justice system itself, including prejudicial sentencing practices, varying treatment within US jails and prisons, and the lack of effective rehabilitation programs for minorities upon their release.

The Sandra Bland case was one of many that have called into question whether race is the root cause of so many injustices. Over time, Bland's family came to terms with the circumstances surrounding her death. State trooper Brian Encinia was fired from the department and faced criminal charges for the way he handled the case.

Court-mandated changes were implemented at the jail where Bland was held. These changes included electronic sensors to enforce frequent cell checks, educational screening courses for employees, and the addition of an on-duty medical technician for all shifts.

In November 2016, Bland's mother accepted a $1.9 million settlement in her wrongful death lawsuit against Waller County officials. The judgment wouldn't bring her daughter back, but she was relieved the case was finally over. "I'm hopeful there won't be any more unlawful arrests," she said. "I'm hopeful with this spotlight and this settlement that others don't have to receive a call from 1,000 miles [1,600 km] away that their child is on the way to the morgue."[8]

| DISCUSSION STARTERS |

- Do you think Sandra Bland was mistreated at Waller County Jail? Why or why not?

- How could Bland's death have been prevented? What measures could be put in place to prevent these events from happening in the future?

- Do you think race plays a defining role in the criminal justice system? Why or why not?

CHAPTER TWO

A NEW CENTURY DIVIDED

The Sentencing Project is an organization dedicated to prison reform in the United States. From 2013 to 2015, the group released a series of studies about the criminal justice system. Among the findings was the fact that, on any given day, one in ten black men in his thirties is behind bars. American Indian youth are three times as likely as white youth to be held in juvenile detention centers. Hispanic men are more than twice as likely to be imprisoned as non-Hispanic white men. Overall, racial and ethnic minorities make up 37 percent of the US population, but they represent 67 percent of the country's prison population.[1]

These figures suggest there are racial disparities in the criminal justice system. But this isn't a new phenomenon. Before understanding how and why racial biases exist in today's court practices and prison culture, it is necessary to take a look back and ask how we got here.

WORKING ON THE CHAIN GANG

For much of the 1900s, hundreds of thousands of Americans, especially black people in the South, were discriminated against because of their race. After the Civil War ended, millions of enslaved people were freed under the Thirteenth Amendment to the US Constitution.

This was a massive societal change that left a gaping hole in the South's economy. White plantation owners— who had depended on slavery for farm labor and other tasks—were left without workers.

Around the same time, Southern African Americans were being arrested in droves and sent to prison for minor crimes. While in prison,

THIRTEENTH AMENDMENT LOOPHOLE?

The Thirteenth Amendment to the US Constitution states, "Neither slavery nor involuntary servitude, except as a punishment for crime whereof the party shall have been duly convicted, shall exist within the United States, or any place subject to their jurisdiction."[2] This amendment formally abolished slavery in 1865. But some historians believe it also left open a loophole allowing courts to interpret the punishment clause more broadly. As a result, they say, prisoners are not covered by the Thirteenth Amendment's protections.

they became part of the convict leasing system. Under this system, the state rented out prisoners to local farmers or industrial companies in exchange for a fee. The farmers or companies housed and fed the convicts; in return, they received cheap labor. Meanwhile, the state boosted its revenue. Soon, buying and selling these leases became a profitable business. "Convict leasing in the South in this period [became] a new way of racial control among white Southerners attempting to limit African American economic independence and freedom in general," said

Prior to the ratification of the Thirteenth Amendment, millions of enslaved black people worked on plantations.

Khalil Muhammad, professor of history, race, and public policy at Harvard Kennedy School. "Once you were in the system, you could spend the rest of your life there."[3]

By the early 1900s, public outcry against the harshness of convict leasing gave rise to a different method of managing the prison population. Instead of private farmers or companies benefiting from convict labor, state governments assumed control. They forced inmates to repair roads or work on other public projects while chained together at the ankle. Some inmates were housed in tiny mobile jail cells and worked long shifts without sufficient food or clothing. "The chain gang initially began as a reform over these terrible abuses that had been going on in the prison system before," said

Douglas A. Blackmon, author of *Slavery by Another Name*. "But immediately [it] became as terrible, infamous, and notorious an institution in the South as convict leasing had been."[4]

African Americans were technically free after the passage of the Thirteenth Amendment. But as members of chain gangs and convict leasing programs, they were still exploited for others' personal and corporate gain. They also faced another pressing challenge: the far reach of a white supremacist group called the Ku Klux Klan.

PUNISHMENT BY LYNCHING

Beginning in the late 1800s and stretching to the beginning of the civil rights movement in the 1950s, states and cities enacted a series of regulations known as Jim Crow laws. These laws were designed to enforce the segregation of minorities—mainly black people—in public areas such as schools, restaurants, restrooms, and buses. As in the past, black people were arrested for wrongdoings both large and small. Some confessed to and were convicted of serious crimes. But others were merely accused of slander, penalized for acting inappropriately toward a white person, or targeted for seeming troublesome. In many cases, they were jailed for crimes they didn't commit.

LYNCH MOB

In 1916, 17-year-old Jesse Washington, who was black, was convicted of killing his white employer's wife in Waco, Texas. Though Washington was promised the court's protection, spectators from the trial took matters into their own hands. They grabbed him from the courtroom and dragged him outside.

In front of a crowd of thousands, Washington was tortured. He was stripped of his clothes, chained to a car, and dragged to city hall. Then he was stabbed, strung up from a tree in front of the mayor's window, and lowered into a fire. A professional photographer took photographs, which were made into postcards. No one was ever prosecuted for the lynching.

Some punishments took place without any action from a government official. Many beatings and lynchings were doled out not by members of a police force, but by the Ku Klux Klan. Most Klansmen were white middle-class Protestants. They dressed in white sheets and triangle-shaped hats. Klansmen primarily despised black people but also hated Jews, Catholics, immigrants, and other groups that threatened their sense of superiority and privilege in US society. White people who were not Klan members sometimes joined in on these beatings and lynchings because they felt angry about the increased presence of freed slaves and the poor economy.

Lynching victims were chased and caught by a mob. Some were strung up from trees and hung. Others were burned alive at the stake. This gruesome behavior was not only condoned by state and federal officials during or after the fact—it was also a public spectacle held in town squares with crowds of thousands looking on. In the grisliest cases, parts of the victim's body were cut off and kept as souvenirs by members of the audience.

A lynching victim hangs from a tree in the 1920s.

Between 1882 and 1968, there were 4,743 reported lynchings in the United States. The true number is likely much higher, as many lynchings went unreported. Of the reported victims, approximately 3,446 were black. The 1,297 white victims were mostly antilynching sympathizers or those trying to protect black people.[5]

SEQUESTERED PEOPLES

Chain gangs and lynching were not the only discriminatory penal measures inflicted on minorities. Throughout the 1800s, the US Army rounded up thousands of American Indians and forcibly relocated them to smaller settlements in the West. Their land rights were seized. Many tribal men, women, and children

THE LEGALITY OF LYNCHING

In 1918, Missouri representative Leonidas C. Dyer introduced antilynching legislation into the US Congress. If Dyer's bill had become law, it would have enacted several mandates. First, members of lynch mobs would be charged with murder, and lynching cases would be tried in federal court. Second, a fine between $5,000 and $10,000 would be imposed on the county where the lynching occurred and paid to the victim's family. Third, state and local law enforcement officials who refused to prevent a lynching would face a mandatory jail sentence and a fine of up to $5,000. Fourth, lynch mob participants or supporters of lynch mobs would be prohibited from serving on a jury.

Though the bill passed in the House of Representatives, it was defeated in the Senate. As of 2017, the United States has not formally passed antilynching legislation.

were jailed or killed for refusing to cooperate. In what was known as the Trail of Tears, more than 5,000 Cherokees died in 1838 on the 1,200-mile (1,900 km) journey from their home in Georgia to Indian Territory in present-day Oklahoma.[6]

During World War II (1939–1945), approximately 120,000 Japanese Americans, two-thirds of whom were US citizens, were held in remote areas throughout the western United States.[7] President Franklin D. Roosevelt had signed an executive order in February 1942 in response to Japan's bombing of Pearl Harbor, Hawaii, two months earlier. Roosevelt's order forced Americans of Japanese descent to relocate to internment camps. These camps resembled prisons, with barbed wire and armed guards. There were

A SIGNED APOLOGY

In 1980, the federal Commission on Wartime Relocation and Internment of Civilians was formed to study the effects of imprisonment on Japanese Americans during World War II. Two years later, the commission released a 467-page report entitled "Personal Justice Denied." The causes of Japanese internment were described as being "motivated largely by racial prejudice, wartime hysteria, and a failure of political leadership." To rectify the situation, Congress passed the Civil Liberties Act in 1988. Commonly known as the Japanese American Redress Bill, this act acknowledged "a grave injustice was done." Congress agreed to pay each internment victim $20,000 in reparations along with providing a signed apology from the president.[8]

Japanese Americans arrive at an internment camp in March 1942.

schools, community centers, and weekly newspapers. Still, conditions were basic, medical care was minimal, and many inmates were malnourished and suffered brutal punishments.

"There was always this feeling, well, what are we in for?" said Bob Fuchigami, speaking about his time at Amache internment camp in Granada, Colorado.

"Why are we in here? What are they going to do to us tomorrow or the next day?"[9]

Whether they were Japanese Americans in the 1940s or African Americans during the past two centuries, members of certain racial and ethnic groups have been systematically targeted throughout US history because of their race. "History is not just stuff that happens by accident," says Kevin Gannon, professor of history at Grand View University. "We are the products of the history our ancestors chose—if we are white. If we are black, we are products of the history our ancestors most likely did not choose. Yet here we are together, the products of that set of choices. And we have to understand that in order to escape the problem."[10]

| DISCUSSION STARTERS |

- Do you think the Thirteenth Amendment was intended to have a loophole? Why or why not? What effect do you think its language has had on black prisoners, who make up a larger percentage of the prison population?

- Many white people in the South were distraught by the failing economy and poor infrastructure at the end of the Civil War. How do you think their attitudes were affected by the large numbers of freed slaves?

CHAPTER THREE

THE WAR ON DRUGS

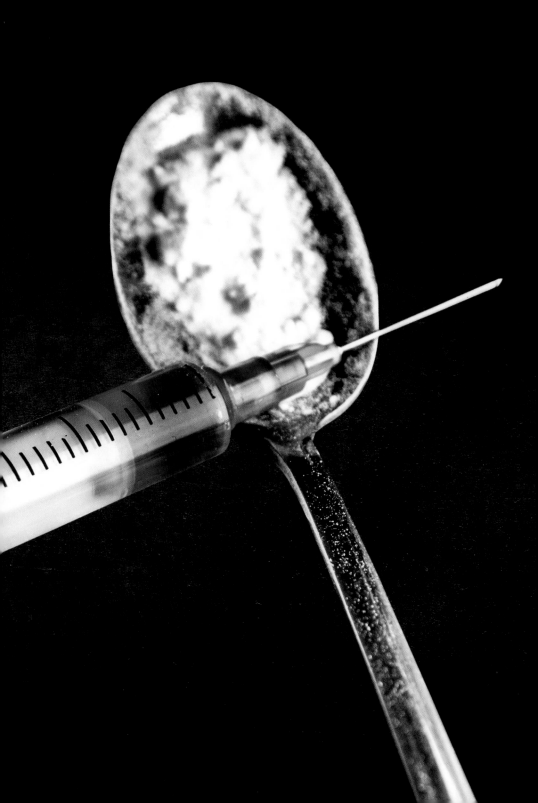

As of 2016, more than half of the inmates in US federal prisons were there because of drug offenses. At the state level, the number of people incarcerated for drug-related crimes is ten times higher than it was in 1980. By the end of 2015, the number had reached nearly 500,000.[1] According to the US Bureau of Justice Statistics, most of these felons have no prior record for a violent criminal offense. Many were arrested on minor charges, such as possession of marijuana.

These inmates are in prison as a result of the country's ongoing war on drugs. As seen in other areas of criminal justice, African Americans, Latinos, and the poor are disproportionately targeted for drug-related offenses. According to the Drug Policy Alliance, African Americans are "more likely to be stopped, searched, arrested, convicted, harshly sentenced and saddled with a lifelong criminal record."[2] A 2016 study found that black people, who make up 13 percent of the US population, use drugs the same amount as other races, including white people. Yet black people make up 31 percent of all drug arrests.[3]

For Latinos, the picture is similar. According to the Drug Policy Alliance, Latinos represent 17 percent of the US population. However, they made up 22 percent of drug arrests in 2014. Latinos make up 20 percent of people in state prisons for drug offenses and 37 percent of inmates in federal prisons for the same crimes.

When these figures are combined, it means nearly 80 percent of people in federal prison and approximately 60 percent of people in state prison for drug offenses are black or Latino.[4] But the trend of incarcerating a larger number of people of color for drug-related crimes is not new. The practice began in the 1970s.

Racial minorities are statistically more likely to face drug arrests.

TOUGH ON DRUGS

In the 1970s, during the presidency of Richard Nixon, the United States was going through a turbulent time. Tens of thousands of people were protesting the country's role in the Vietnam War (1955–1975). The movements for civil rights, women's liberation, and gay rights were going strong. Federal spending for local law enforcement had doubled. At the same time, Nixon was waging a battle against drugs. Marijuana was included with heroin and cocaine as a Schedule I drug, meaning it was among the most dangerous controlled substances.

Nixon also cracked down on drug dealers. He turned drug use from a health issue into a crime issue—one that required tough, strict measures. Many of his targets were black people. In 1994, John Ehrlichman, an adviser to Nixon, said:

> The Nixon campaign in 1968, and the Nixon White House after that, had two enemies: the anti-war left and black people. . . . We knew we couldn't make it illegal to be either against the war or black, but by getting the public to associate the hippies with marijuana and blacks with heroin, and then criminalizing both heavily, we could disrupt those communities. . . . Did we know we were lying about the drugs? Of course we did.[5]

A drug dealer sells crack on the streets of New York City in the 1980s.

Nevertheless, many Americans were genuinely concerned about the influence of drugs on society. In a 1986 poll, 42 percent of respondents said crack was the most dangerous drug in the country.[6] The same year, 54 percent of inmates at state prisons reported they were under the influence of drugs or alcohol at the time of their crimes.[7] To address the public's fears, many politicians felt they had to create tougher laws. In 1986, President Ronald Reagan signed the Anti-Drug Abuse Act, which established a mandatory five-year minimum sentence for possession of five grams of crack. This cheaper form of smokable cocaine was most commonly used by black people and poor people in inner-city neighborhoods. In contrast, users of powdered cocaine—who were mostly

THE SCHOOL-TO-PRISON PIPELINE

On September 14, 1986, First Lady Nancy Reagan appeared on television and repeated a phrase that would soon become famous across the country: *Just say no.* She urged American kids, teens, and parents to refuse drugs and alcohol.

However, many experts say the campaign didn't work. Instead, it gave rise to a phenomenon known as the school-to-prison pipeline. In 1986, Congress passed the Drug-Free Schools and Communities Act. It mandated zero tolerance for any drugs or alcohol on school property. This policy brought police officers into schools. As a result, officers started arresting students.

Similar to their adult counterparts, black and Latino teens were more likely to be suspended from school or arrested for drug or alcohol infractions. Once in jail, tasks such as graduating from high school and landing a job became far more difficult. Many never made it out of the prison cycle.

white, wealthy, and lived in the suburbs—had to be caught with at least 500 grams to receive the same minimum sentence.[8]

The Anti-Drug Abuse Act effectively created both an economic and a racial divide in sentencing guidelines for the same drug. It was also the first time the federal government established a mandatory minimum sentence for a drug offense. Consequently, rich white people stayed out of prison while impoverished black people and other minorities were arrested and imprisoned for lengthy terms. "In many ways, the so-called war on drugs was a war on communities of color, a

war on black communities, a war on Latino communities,"
said Angela Davis, a political activist and professor at the
University of California, Santa Cruz.[9]

MASS INCARCERATION

As a result of the mass incarceration of drug offenders, the
US prison population ballooned to nearly 1.8 million
by the 1990s. Among the total prison population, the
number of people incarcerated for nonviolent drug crimes
was approximately 50,000 in 1980; by 1997, the number
had reached more than 400,000.[10] Instead of probation,
more first-time drug offenders received a prison term.
They were put away for longer amounts of time. Penalties
doubled for those arrested a second time. Those arrested
a third time, or those who were caught in possession of
large amounts of drugs at any point, were sentenced to life
in prison without the possibility of parole. This policy was
known as the Three Strikes Law.

By the mid-2010s, the trend had begun to sound
alarms. Many lawmakers felt increasingly uneasy about the
impact the war on drugs was having on black and Latino
communities. "We are a nation that professes freedom
yet have this mass incarceration, this hyper-incarceration
system . . . that is grinding into it our most vulnerable
citizenry—and is overwhelmingly biased towards people

A SECOND CHANCE

Ismael Rosa, a Hispanic man, is a salsa singer and a father of five living in Chicago, Illinois. In 1995, he was arrested for possessing multiple kilograms of cocaine. Though he had been on probation twice before for drugs, he had never been in prison. But because of the Three Strikes Law, he received a life sentence. Rosa was a model prisoner for the many years he was incarcerated. He took classes and ran the prison's barbershop. He never thought he would get out. But on March 30, 2016, after serving 21 years, President Obama pardoned him. Rosa told his lawyer, "Please tell Mr. President that I will always represent him and I will not let him down."[13]

of color," said Cory Booker, a US senator from New Jersey.[11]

The incarceration of minorities for nonviolent drug offenses also had a devastating effect on families and neighborhoods. According to a report issued by the Drug Policy Alliance in 2016, one in nine black children had a parent behind bars, compared to one in 28 Latino children and one in 57 white children.[12] A drug conviction can mean losing a child to foster care; the rejection of a job application or business loan; and the loss of student aid, public housing, or other public assistance.

In recent years, a movement to reform the Three Strikes Law and other strict drug laws has been underway. In the 2010s, President Barack Obama worked with members of Congress to overturn some of the minimum sentencing laws established in the 1980s and 1990s. He also commuted the sentences of more than 1,100 nonviolent drug offenders—more than the previous 11 presidents combined. Approximately one-third of these recipients were serving life sentences.[14]

"We must remember that these are individuals—sons, daughters, parents, and in many cases, grandparents—who have taken steps toward rehabilitation and who have earned their second chance," said White House counsel Neil Eggleston in 2016. "They are individuals who received unduly harsh sentences under outdated laws for committing largely nonviolent drug crimes."[15]

DISCUSSION STARTERS

- How have mandatory minimum sentences and the Three Strikes Law affected the prison population in the United States? How have they affected black and Latino communities?

- President Obama commuted many drug offenders' sentences in 2016. Do you think this was a good idea? Why or why not?

- Other than sending nonviolent drug offenders to prison, can you think of any other ways to reduce drug use in the United States?

PRISONS TURNING A PROFIT

According to the US Bureau of Justice Statistics, the American criminal justice system contains approximately 1,719 state prisons, 102 federal prisons, 942 juvenile correctional facilities, 3,283 local jails, and 79 Indian country jails. In addition, the criminal justice system includes military prisons and immigration detention facilities. These are funded primarily by taxpayer dollars. Of all the country's prisoners, approximately 8 percent are housed in for-profit prisons. Many of these private prisons are run by a company called Corrections Corporation of America (CCA).[16]

Critics of CCA rally outside a detention facility in Elizabeth, New Jersey.

In the early 1980s, the war on drugs resulted in mass incarceration. In response, CCA established itself in 1983 as a company that could answer the need for more state and federal prisons. CCA claimed it could build and operate these facilities with the same quality of service as government-run prisons but at a lower cost. In reality, this claim proved to be untrue. CCA's prisons were often more violent than their government-run counterparts.

In August 2016, the Obama administration announced it would begin to reduce the use of for-profit prisons. The Bureau of Prisons was projected to house only 14,200 inmates in private prisons by May 2017, down from approximately 30,000 in 2013.[17]

IMMIGRATION AND THE CRIMINAL JUSTICE SYSTEM

Chan Om was just a child when he arrived in Minnesota in the 1970s. He and others had made the journey from Cambodia to escape the atrocities that were taking place as a result of the Vietnam War. During that period, more than 150,000 Cambodians sought legal asylum in the United States.

But on August 26, 2016, Om's life changed for the worse. Now 46 years old, Om drove to a US Immigration and Customs Enforcement (ICE) office for his regular check-in. When he got there, he was detained. After more than three decades of living in the United States, he faced deportation back to Cambodia.

Om is a former criminal. In 2004, he and others tried to rob a local restaurant. They were arrested, and Om served more than three years in prison. Though he found a home and a job after he got out, Om could be sent back to his birth country because of an agreement the United States struck with Cambodia in 2002. The agreement stated that any refugee with a criminal record could be deported at any time no matter when the crime was committed, even if he or she was in the United States legally.

Studies have shown that immigrants such as Om are less likely to commit violent crimes than their second- or third-generation counterparts. Still, they often face insurmountable challenges when trying to forge new lives in a new country. Paul Lelii, a lawyer who works with cases such as Om's, said the situation is stacked against them. "They're the children of people who assisted this country," he said. "We brought them here. The last thing we should be doing is sending their children back to the place we saved them from."[1]

A DIFFERENCE IN DEFINITION

Many people believe undocumented immigrants, particularly those convicted of crimes, should be deported. Supporters of this viewpoint say deportation would make the country safer. ICE has been especially vigilant in detaining nonwhite drug offenders and those who have been convicted of a crime. According to

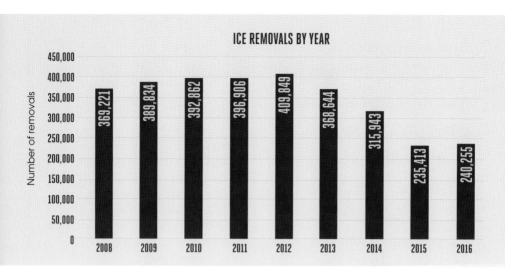

ICE REMOVALS BY YEAR

Year	Number of removals
2008	369,221
2009	389,834
2010	392,862
2011	396,906
2012	409,849
2013	368,644
2014	315,943
2015	235,413
2016	240,255

The majority of deportations are of undocumented immigrants who were previously convicted of a crime.

data released by the Pew Research Center, there are approximately 11.1 million unauthorized immigrants in the United States. Of that number, 139,368 were deported in 2015 for being convicted criminals.[3] The largest portions were from Mexico, Guatemala, and other Central American countries.

However, many experts say the definition of "convicted criminal" means something different in the matter of immigration. "Immigrants who experience even the slightest brush with the criminal justice system, such as being convicted of a misdemeanor, can find themselves subject to detention for an undetermined period, after which they are expelled from the country and barred from returning," says Walter Ewing, a senior researcher for the

American Immigration Council (AIC). "In other words, for years the government has been redefining what it means to be a 'criminal alien,' using increasingly stringent definitions and standards of 'criminality' that do not apply to US citizens."[4]

Since the late 1800s, the US Supreme Court has classified deportation as a civil act. This means deportation is technically considered an administrative decision rather than a form of punishment.

Deported immigrants stage a protest at the US–Mexico border to call for an end to abuses by border police.

Undocumented immigrants are not entitled to the same constitutional rights as US citizens. For instance, they are not read their rights when they are arrested. However, in some cases they can file motions to suppress incriminating statements. They are not provided with an attorney during interrogations but can choose not to make a statement.

Undocumented immigrants who have not been deported before can appear before an immigration judge. If they are eligible for immigration relief, they can challenge their deportation. In most cases, they do not qualify for any relief and must accept their fate of deportation to their country of birth. Deportation often results in them being separated from their family and friends. In addition, their lives might be in danger when they return to their country of birth, as others may assume they have a lot of money because they lived in the United States.

RIGHTS OF NONCITIZEN IMMIGRANTS

In the criminal justice system, most crimes are subject to statutes of limitation. This means after a designated period of time, the government is not allowed to prosecute perpetrators of certain crimes. Statutes of limitation force law enforcement to make speedy arrests of suspects and the government to make swift decisions whether to prosecute those suspects. Certain crimes are not subject to the statutes of limitation; those who are suspected of heinous crimes can always be prosecuted, irrespective of when they are arrested. Statutes of limitation do not apply to immigrants in deportation proceedings. Therefore, ICE can start deportation proceedings against noncitizens decades after they entered the United States unlawfully, overstayed their visit, or were convicted of a serious crime.

In addition, noncitizen immigrants do not receive pretrial hearings to determine whether their arrest was justified or whether they will be

A 30-YEAR THREAT OF DEPORTATION

In 1970, 11-year-old Juan Rivas-Melendrez left Mexico to come to the United States. He entered with a green card, a legal document that certified he was a lawful permanent resident. Ten years later, when he was 21, he was arrested for having sex with his 17-year-old girlfriend. The sex was consensual, but Rivas-Melendrez was convicted of statutory rape because his partner was under the age of 18.

Rivas-Melendrez later served in the US Army. After that, he got married and started a family. The couple had four children, all of whom were citizens because they were born in the United States.

But Rivas-Melendrez's situation changed in 2009. The Department of Homeland Security became aware of his decades-old conviction and initiated deportation proceedings. "Because of the lack of a statute of limitations on the grounds of deportability, someone like Rivas-Melendrez can be removed from his home and family at any point," said an AIC report.[5]

An ICE officer arrests suspected undocumented immigrants.

allowed bail. This step is customary in most criminal

cases involving citizens. Instead, immigrants are given

a mandatory detention sentence—which can last for

weeks, months, or even years—while they await their deportation hearing.

The United States has the capacity to hold 34,000 noncitizens in more than 200 civil detention facilities across the country, including private detention centers, county jails, and a few federal prisons.[6] A 2015 report by the US Commission on Civil Rights states a majority of these facilities are overcrowded and filthy. Health care is minimal. Guards look the other way in cases of sexual abuse or rape. Some detainees find the conditions to be so restrictive that they commit suicide rather than wait for a trial and the slim chance of freedom.

"We have witnessed the creation of an environment which condones the inhumane treatment of immigrants, especially those coming from Latin America," wrote commission chairman Martin R. Castro.[7]

The AIC suggests the US immigration policy is "broken." This organization, along

DYING IN CUSTODY

From 2003 to 2016, approximately 160 immigrants died while in ICE's custody awaiting deportation proceedings. They were being held in detention centers such as the Eloy Detention Center in Arizona, which houses up to 1,600 immigrants on any given day. Eloy is one of more than 200 immigration detention facilities located in the United States. Of the seven suicides of ICE detainees between 2005 and 2015, five took place at Eloy, including that of 31-year-old José de Jesús Deniz Sahagun. "This was a man who . . . had a family that he missed terribly," said Dr. Allen Keller, director of a New York University program for survivors of torture. "He had not been a danger to our country. And in the equation, it got lost that this was a human being."[8]

with other groups, has been calling for reform, and the demands are getting louder. "In reforming our immigration system," the AIC states, "we must not forget that the immigration removal system—from arrest to hearing to deportation and beyond—does not reflect American values of due process and fundamental fairness."[9]

However, Donald Trump's victory in the 2016 presidential election led many observers to believe immigration reform was unlikely. Experts predicted President Trump would vigorously enforce existing immigration laws.

DISCUSSION STARTERS

- Should noncitizen immigrants receive the same rights as US citizens, even if they are criminals? Why or why not?

- Do you think Latinos are disproportionately affected by US immigration laws? Why or why not?

- Many children are born in the United States but have parents who are undocumented immigrants. Other children born in the United States have parents who have a green card but have not yet obtained full citizenship. What impact do current immigration laws have on these children?

CHAPTER FIVE

THE SCOURGE IN SENTENCING

In 2013, author and civil rights activist Michelle Alexander was interviewed about her book *The New Jim Crow*. During the interview, she discussed the war on drugs, the mass incarceration of people of color, and what effect racially discriminatory practices might have on the United States in the future. "I think most Americans have no idea of the scale and scope of mass incarceration in the United States," she told the reporter. "Unless you're directly impacted by the system, unless you have a loved one who's behind bars, unless you've done time yourself . . . it's hard to even imagine that something of this scope and scale could even exist."[1]

JUSTICE, AT A PRICE

In 2016, there were approximately 2.3 million incarcerated people in the United States. The cost of housing, feeding, managing, and maintaining the health of these prisoners is high. According to figures released by the Federal Bureau of Prisons, an inmate housed in the federal prison system costs the US government an average of $30,619.85 per year. That comes out to $83.89 per prisoner per day.[2]

According to Alexander, there are more black people in prison, in jail, on probation, or on parole today than were enslaved in 1850 prior to the Civil War. Much of the reason for this, she and others believe, is because of sentencing biases.

In 2014, the American Civil Liberties

Union (ACLU) sent a report to the Inter-American Commission on Human Rights citing "significant racial disparities" in the US criminal justice system's sentencing practices. The study showed African American and Latino offenders sentenced in state and federal courts were more likely to be incarcerated than white people accused of similar crimes. The report also stated that sentences imposed on black men in federal cases were nearly 20 percent longer than those given to white men who had committed the same crimes.[3]

In addition, the ACLU findings suggested racial disparities increased with the severity of the sentence imposed. For example, African Americans made up 13 percent of the US population in 2009. Using the data provided in the study, African Americans represented

UNEQUAL
PRISON SENTENCES

A 2012 report from the University of Michigan Law School showed that white people tend to receive significantly shorter sentences than black people. For example, 53 percent of white people received sentences of 25 months or fewer; only 30 percent of black people received similar sentences. In contrast, only 6 percent of white people received sentences of 175 months or longer, while 12 percent of black people received similar sentences. The report indicated that, on average, black people received sentences that were 10 percent longer than the sentences of white people.[4]

Studies indicate that black people spend longer in prison than white people who are convicted of similar crimes.

28 percent of all people in prison for life that same year, 56 percent of those serving life without the possibility of parole, and 56 percent of those who received life without parole for crimes committed as a young person. In the first-ever study of people serving life without parole for nonviolent offenses, conducted by the ACLU in 2013, 65 percent were African American, compared to 18 percent white and 16 percent Latino.[5]

"The people profiled in our report are an extreme example of the millions of lives ruined by the persistent ratcheting up of our sentencing laws over the last 40 years," said Vanita Gupta, deputy legal director of the ACLU. "We must change our sentencing practices to make our justice system smart, fair, and humane."[6]

PLEA BARGAINS: GOOD OR BAD?

When a person is arrested for a crime and is facing jail time, two things can happen. One, he or she can take the case to court, plead either guilty or not guilty, and let a jury decide his or her fate. Or, two, the person can accept a plea bargain. Plea bargains are deals negotiated by lawyers, in which the individual being accused—the defendant—agrees to plead guilty in exchange for a reduced charge.

Sometimes, as in the case of a serial offender who admits he is guilty, a plea bargain can be an opportunity for a shorter sentence. In other

RACE AND PLEA BARGAIN RATES IN NEW YORK CITY

In 2014, the Vera Institute of Justice examined more than 220,000 cases handled by the Manhattan district attorney's office during 2010 and 2011. The researchers discovered that race played "a statistically significant independent factor" in the way cases were handled at nearly every stage. Here are some of the findings:

- African Americans were 19 percent more likely than whites to be offered plea bargains that included jail or prison time.

- African Americans and Latinos were both more likely than whites to be offered plea bargains that included jail time for minor drug offenses. For marijuana cases specifically, African Americans were 19 percent more likely to be offered a plea bargain that required jail or prison time.

- For non-marijuana felony drug offenses, Latinos were 14 percent more likely than whites to receive plea bargains that required time behind bars.[7]

situations, however, problems arise when the accused insists he or she isn't guilty but is pressured to take a deal anyway. This is what happened to Kalief Browder, and the result was catastrophic.

In 2010, the 16-year-old African American was arrested for the first time for a robbery he claimed he didn't take part in. Bail was set at $10,000, but Browder couldn't pay it. He was offered a plea bargain, but he didn't take it. Instead, he was sent to Rikers Island prison complex in New York City, where he spent more than 1,000 days waiting for a trial that never occurred. Nearly two years of that time was spent in solitary confinement. Guards beat him severely and repeatedly, and he tried to kill himself several times. In May 2013, the case against Browder was dismissed, and he was released from custody. But by then, the damage had already been done. He committed suicide on June 6, 2015.

JURY SELECTION AND WHITE PROSECUTORS

Browder's situation was an extreme case. But going to trial can have mixed results, especially in cases involving the death penalty. On many occasions, the system works as it is meant to. But in other instances, defendants—particularly nonwhite defendants—face predominantly white juries with preexisting racial biases. This can

Activists demonstrate outside New York City Hall to voice their belief that racist policies at Rikers Island led to the death of Kalief Browder.

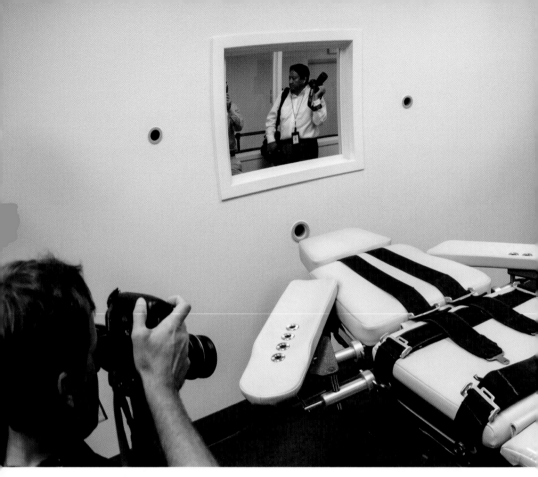

All-white juries tend to give nonwhite defendants a disproportionate number of death sentences, which are often carried out by lethal injection.

potentially affect the trial's outcome. One example is the case of *Foster v. Chatman*.

In 1987, 18-year-old African American Timothy Foster was arrested and tried for murdering Queen Madge White, a 79-year-old white woman in Georgia. Foster was convicted by an all-white jury and sentenced to death. But in 2016, after a series of appeals, the US Supreme Court ordered a retrial on the basis of racially discriminatory jury selection practices. According to the court's findings,

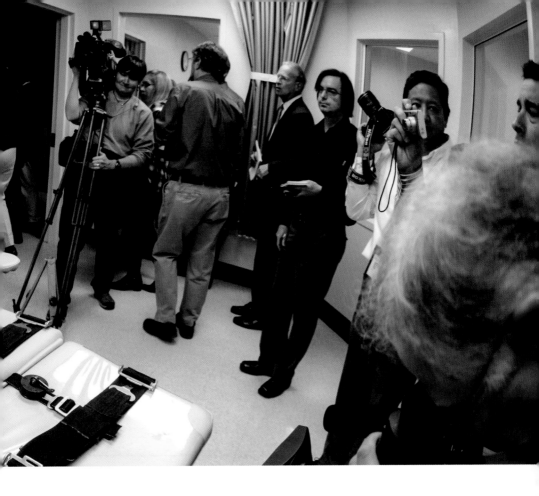

four jurors were purposefully barred from serving because they were black. "This discrimination became apparent only because we obtained the prosecution's notes which revealed their intent to discriminate," said Stephen Bright, Foster's lead lawyer from the Southern Center for Human Rights.[8]

Bright went on to say the practice of using race as a determining factor for filtering jury pools was a common practice across the country. Normally, he said, courts ignore patterns of race discrimination and accept false reasons for any removals. A study of death penalty juries in Houston County, Alabama, proved this to be true. It revealed 80 percent of qualified African Americans were cut from juries. As a result, in a county where 27 percent of the population was black, most juries for death penalty cases consisted exclusively of white people. Another study in North Carolina found that from 1990 to 2010, prosecutors excluded African American jurors twice as often as jurors of any other race.[9]

In many cases, it's not only the jury pool but also a disproportionate number of lawyers who are white. As of July 2015, there were more than 2,400 prosecutors in the United States. Ninety-five percent of them were white and 83 percent were men, according to the findings from the Reflective Democracy Campaign, a project of the Women Donors Network. Only 1 percent were women of color. In 13 states, the pool of prosecutors was 100 percent white.[10]

A large proportion of people who are convicted of crimes in the United States, the majority of whom are black, are tried by people of a different race—mainly white people. While this may not present a problem in most situations, in some instances racial biases might influence a jury's decision or a prosecutor's ability to present the best possible defense. "I think most people know that we've had a significant problem with lack of diversity in decision-making roles in the criminal justice system for a long time," said Bryan A. Stevenson, founder of the Equal Justice Initiative, an organization that offers legal representation to poor defendants and prisoners.[11]

In an interview in the *New York Times*, Brenda Choresi Carter of the Women Donors Network agreed. "What [it] shows us is that, in the context of a growing crisis that we all recognize in criminal justice in this country, we have a system where incredible power and discretion is concentrated in the hands of one demographic group," she said.[12]

| DISCUSSION STARTERS |

- What are some possible effects of racial discrimination in the jury selection process?

- If you were accused of a crime you didn't commit, would you take a plea bargain in exchange for a shorter sentence? Why or why not?

- In 1987, Thomas Foster was found guilty of murder and put on death row. Do you think he deserved a new trial, given that the verdict was delivered by an all-white jury? Why or why not?

CHAPTER SIX

BEHIND BARS

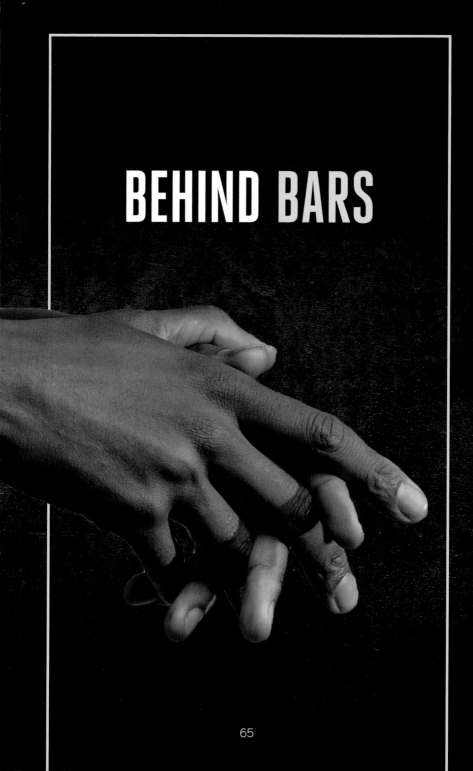

On August 4, 2010, 24-year-old Rocrast Mack Jr. was lying in his prison cot preparing for sleep. Mack, who is black, had been convicted of drug possession and sentenced to 20 years at Ventress Correctional Facility in Clayton, Alabama. One of the prison's guards, officer Melissa Brown, was doing a routine check in Mack's prison block.

When Brown entered Mack's cell, she thought he looked at her inappropriately. In response, Brown yelled at Mack and hit him in the face twice. When he tried to defend himself, she chased him out of the cell where another officer was waiting. Mack was ordered to kneel on the ground with his hands behind his head. He willingly complied. By that time, at least five other officers had arrived as backup. They kicked and beat Mack on his head and body with their batons and fists until Mack lost consciousness. Then they slammed his head into a wall. By the time the assault was complete, Mack was brain-dead. Dozens of inmates witnessed the act.

The violence inflicted upon Mack by correctional officers is not an anomaly in today's prison system. Twenty-one percent of all men in US prisons say they have been attacked by a staff member.[1] And these are only the reported cases. These statistics—combined with inmate-on-inmate violence and the rising death toll due to disease, drug or alcohol abuse, and suicide—make prisons and jails difficult and, at times, unsafe places to be.

A RACIAL DISCREPANCY

According to a 2015 study by the Center for American Progress, one in three black males born in 2001 will go to prison at some point during his life. One in six Latino males will face the same fate. In contrast, one of every 17 white males is expected to end up in prison.[2]

Approximately 67 percent of the US prison population is people of color.[3] In contrast, most US prisons are staffed by a majority of white correctional officers. During the 1990s and into the 2000s, the United States saw a boom in prison construction, with most being built in rural areas. Because these facilities were located in largely white neighborhoods, the majority of the people hired as guards

A RISING DEATH TOLL

Since 2000, when the US Bureau of Justice Statistics started keeping track of the death rate in local jails and state prisons, the number of deaths has steadily risen. Between 2012 and 2013, the number of inmate deaths increased from 4,315 to 4,446. This is the highest number of deaths recorded since data collection began. Illness-related mortalities accounted for 89 percent of all deaths in prison in 2013, while suicide has been the leading cause of death in jails every year since 2000.[4]

A white prison guard puts a black inmate into his cell.

were also white. This was in stark contrast to the prison population, in which a majority of inmates were nonwhite.

As an example, African Americans and Latinos made up approximately 76 percent of New York's prison population in 2005. In that same year, they represented less than 12 percent of prison staff positions. The disparity was reflected nationwide as well.[5] These statistics meant nonwhite prisoners were likely to be watched over or punished by white guards. The same disproportionate ratio still held true as of 2017.

WOMEN IN SHACKLES

Though men make up a majority of the US prison population, the number of incarcerated women has increased by more than 700 percent since 1980. This change was caused in part by stricter drug enforcement practices, harsher sentencing policies, and lengthier sentence terms. As of 2014, there were more than 215,000 women behind bars and approximately 1 million on probation or parole. Black women were twice as likely as white women to be incarcerated, while Hispanic women were jailed at 1.2 times the rate of white women.[6] According to a 2015 study by the Center for American Progress, one in 18 black women born in 2001 will go to prison at some point during her life. In contrast, one in

AN ONGOING INVESTIGATION

For women convicted of crimes, one of the worst places to be sent is Julia Tutwiler Prison for Women in Wetumpka, Alabama. According to an ongoing investigation conducted by the US Justice Department, guards have taunted, beaten, and raped female inmates there for at least 18 years. More than one-third of its correction officers have had sex with prisoners, often in exchange for doling out an extra roll of toilet paper. But Tutwiler is not the only problem prison in the state. "We need to rectify the crimes that happened at Tutwiler," said Cam Ward, a state senator, in 2014. "But going forward it's a bigger problem than just Tutwiler. We're dealing with a box of dynamite."[7]

45 Latina women and one in 111 white women will go to prison.[8]

Women are being incarcerated at a rapid rate—most of the time for minor offenses such as shoplifting, marijuana possession, or failing a drug test while on probation. According to a 2016 report released by the Vera Institute of Justice, the majority of female inmates are poor, black or Hispanic, and have drug or alcohol problems. Approximately 80 percent of them, many of whom are single parents, have children at home. "As the focus on [smaller] crimes has increased, women have been swept up into the system to an even greater extent than men," said Elizabeth Swavola, one of the authors of the report.[9]

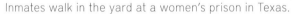

Inmates walk in the yard at a women's prison in Texas.

Female inmates often face taunting and abuse from guards. In some prisons, feminine hygiene products are not free, and they cost more than inmates can afford when earning, on average, only 93 cents a day. At York Correctional Institution in Connecticut, cellmates receive a maximum of five sanitary napkins per week to split. In 2014, the ACLU of Michigan filed a lawsuit on behalf of eight female prisoners claiming the "inhuman and degrading policies at the filthy, overcrowded lockup violate their constitutional rights."[10]

Pregnant women in state prisons are subjected to an even bigger problem:

ATTICA: THEN AND NOW

On September 9, 1971, a massive uprising took place at Attica Correctional Facility in New York. A group of prisoners attempted to take control of the prison to protest its conditions—first through peaceful requests for reform, then by force. At the time, beatings were commonplace. Inmates were allowed only one roll of toilet paper per month and one shower per week. They were put in solitary confinement for sometimes years at a time, often receiving little food. Muslims were prohibited from practicing their religion.

The Attica rebellion lasted three days. On the fourth day, Governor Nelson Rockefeller sent in armed state troopers. Thirty-nine people died, including ten guards. When the attack was over, state corrections commissioner Russell G. Oswald agreed to 28 of the inmates' original demands, some of which are still enforced. As of 2016, for example, there are more than 160 chaplains employed in New York's prisons, including priests, ministers, rabbis, and imams. But one reform measure, to increase the racial diversity of staff, went largely ignored.

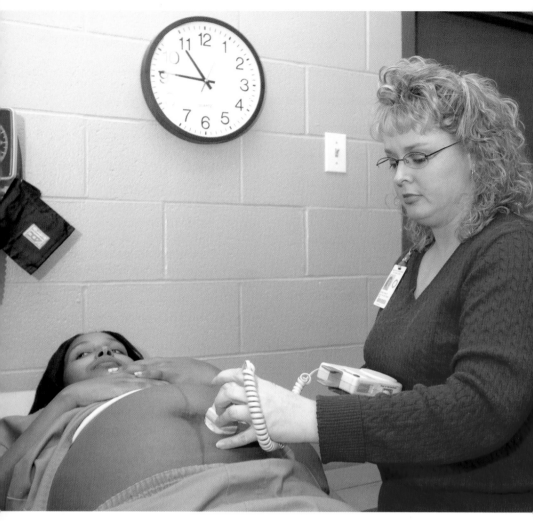

Nikisha Robinson, who is serving a 15-year prison sentence, receives a checkup during her pregnancy.

delivering their babies. Prenatal vitamins are a scarce commodity. Although the Federal Bureau of Prisons passed a law in 2008 barring the use of restraints on inmates who are in labor, some state facilities have ignored the policy. In 2014, former convict Nicole Guerrero filed a lawsuit against Texas's Wichita County Jail, where she was incarcerated for violating her parole. Guerrero was left alone for 12 hours to deliver her baby, Myrah, on the floor of a cramped medical cell. The baby died because the umbilical cord was wrapped around its neck. Guerrero claimed if a guard had been there, the death would not have happened. "All I know is Myrah didn't deserve [to die]," Guerrero said.[11]

For prisoners of both sexes and all races, life behind bars can be incredibly difficult and sometimes life threatening. But the inmates who do manage to get out are not always free. They face an equally difficult challenge: staying out and relearning how to get by.

| DISCUSSION STARTERS |

- How might the racial divide between correction officers and inmates have a negative impact on the prison population? In what ways might the officers and inmates be negatively affected?

- In many prisons, women do not have access to enough feminine hygiene products. In what ways might this affect prisoners? Is this discrimination the same or different than the situation in men's prisons?

CHAPTER SEVEN

POST-PRISON PREJUDICE

EMPLOYM

PERSONAL INFORMATION

Name (Last, First, Middle)

Address

Serving time in prison is difficult. Incarcerated people are separated from society and their families for long periods of time. Some are beaten by corrections officers or fellow inmates during their terms. Others spend long stretches in solitary confinement and develop debilitating psychiatric problems or post-traumatic stress disorder.

But for many convicts, getting out of prison and rebuilding their lives can be just as challenging. According to the US Department of Justice, approximately 600,000 people return to their communities every year after serving time in federal and state prisons. An additional 11.4 million people serve time in local jails.[1] Approximately 47 percent of the prisoners released are African American, 16 percent are Hispanic, and 35 percent are white, according to the American Sociological Association. People of color make up more than two-thirds of returning prisoners.[2] Most are uneducated or undereducated, lack necessary skills, and are not prepared for reentry into society. For this newly freed population, readjusting to life on the outside presents its own set of problems.

People convicted of crimes are often discriminated against when they are released and seeking employment. In most states, job applications require people to disclose any criminal record. As a result, many former convicts feel discouraged from applying to positions they might be suited for. In addition, some employers have policies against hiring candidates with past convictions.

Women and people of color who do manage to get jobs may also face wage discrepancies. Following release from prison, African American ex-convicts face a 21 percent slower rate of wage growth compared to whites in the same situation, according to research from the Center for American Progress.[3] A number of states also have bans on allowing a worker with a felony conviction to be employed in health-service jobs such as nursing, child care, and home health care. These are all areas in which women, particularly poor ones, are disproportionately concentrated.

BAN THE BOX

In 2004, the San Francisco advocacy group All of Us or None started the Ban the Box campaign. Its mission is to inspire the government to enact federal legislation that would remove the conviction history question from job applications. As of October 2016, 150 cities and counties in 24 states have adopted these policies. "Racial disparities exist at every stage of the criminal justice system," wrote Dorsey Nun of the group Prisoners with Children. "Removing barriers to reentry is not just good policy; it is also about human and civil rights, and affording people basic dignity as they seek to support themselves and their families."[4]

In addition, felons might have trouble gaining access to driver's licenses, business loans, welfare checks, or food stamps after they are released. Across 12 states, 180,000 women with drug convictions have been banned for life from receiving cash welfare assistance.[5] The lack of welfare coupled with the difficulties of finding work makes it nearly impossible for these women to support themselves, let alone a family if they have one. Some resort to selling drugs again to earn money, and they often end up back in the criminal justice system when they are caught. But perhaps the most far-reaching effect of a criminal record has to do with voting. It, too, disproportionally affects minorities.

VOTER DISENFRANCHISEMENT

According to the Sentencing Project, 6.1 million Americans are prohibited from voting due to laws that disenfranchise, or exclude, citizens convicted of a felony. The laws vary state by state, with 48 states enacting some form of restriction as of 2016. Several states take an especially restrictive approach by barring all prisoners and all ex-convicts from voting. Only two states do not restrict people's right to vote when they are behind bars.[6]

Many people believe convicted criminals should not have the right to vote. "When someone commits a crime, he commits it not just against the victim, but against our entire society," writes attorney George Brooks in the Fordham Urban Law Journal.[7] However, research indicates that felony disenfranchisement policies have a greater impact on communities of color. For example, compared to the rest of the US population, African Americans are more than four times more likely to lose their voting rights. In the states of Kentucky, Virginia, Tennessee, and Florida, more than 20 percent of African American adults cannot vote. Throughout the country, one out of every 13 black adults—amounting to 2.2 million people—is disenfranchised.[8] Consequently, people from communities where convictions are high, which are often minority neighborhoods in the inner cities, are vastly underrepresented when it comes to deciding on laws

VOTING RESTRICTIONS PLACED ON FELONS AND EX-FELONS

In the United States, voting restrictions placed on incarcerated people vary from state to state. As of 2016, two states—Maine and Vermont—do not restrict the voting rights of anyone with a felony conviction, including those in prison. In 14 states, restrictions are placed on those in prison. In four states—California, New York, Colorado, and Connecticut—restrictions are placed not only on those in prison but also those on parole. An additional 18 states place restrictions on those in prison, on parole, and on probation. Twelve states do not allow anyone with a felony conviction, past or present, to vote.[9]

The right to vote allows citizens to influence the laws that affect their lives.

that might benefit them and their families. The effect can be devastating.

"Denying someone the right to vote says to them: 'You are no longer one of us. You're not a citizen. Your voice doesn't count,'" says Michelle Alexander, author of *The New Jim Crow*. "We can't pretend that this system that we devised is really about public safety or serving the interests of those we claim to represent. . . . It's more about control, power, the relegation of some of us to a second-class status."[10]

A WIN ON HOUSING

Affordable housing is another issue that former prisoners often struggle with. When searching for a place to live after their release, most ex-convicts find the process to be grueling. Some stay with family members until they can get back on their feet. But due to circumstances surrounding their arrests, others are required to find new accommodations right away. Many of these people face significant financial barriers, such as coming up with money to pay the first month's rent. With no other options, some ex-cons resort to living on the street.

In the 2010s, the Obama administration took steps to address this matter. The Fair Housing Act of 1968, which shields renters from discrimination by landlords, included a clause that denied criminals these protections. But in

DEAD-END HOUSING SEARCH

At the age of 22, Pedro Collazo was sent to prison for his role in a deadly bar brawl. He was charged with manslaughter and served 12 years in New York's Sing Sing prison. Upon his release, he found a job so he could support his 12-year-old daughter and 16-year-old son. But housing was another story. After nine months, Collazo still slept on a family member's couch. Landlords routinely turned him away because of his criminal background. "The most recent attempt to secure an apartment was the most overt form of discrimination I have experienced thus far," he said in 2016.[11]

2016, the White House released revised guidelines for the law. These guidelines directly affected minorities with a criminal history:

> Because of widespread racial and ethnic disparities in the US criminal justice system, criminal history-based restrictions on access to housing are likely disproportionately to burden African Americans and Hispanics. [Therefore], while the Act does not prohibit housing providers from appropriately considering criminal history information when making housing decisions, arbitrary and overbroad criminal history-related bans are likely to lack a legally sufficient justification.[12]

The guidelines essentially made it more difficult for landlords to get away with blatant discrimination because of a criminal background. The Obama administration's actions were a small win in the reentry reform movement. Another area where small inroads are being made is education.

ACCESS TO EDUCATION

In 1994, the US Congress passed the Violent Crime Control and Law Enforcement Act. This law banned incarcerated people from receiving federal Pell Grants—financial aid that doesn't have to be paid back—to

President Obama, *center*, spoke to corrections officers when he visited an Oklahoma prison in 2015.

use toward educational purposes. The authors of the legislation believed federal aid was better spent on law-abiding students than those who had been convicted of crimes. As a result of the law, most inmates no longer had access to classes, textbooks, or any materials that might help them obtain an associate's or other college degree while behind bars. Many ex-convicts, a large proportion of them minorities, therefore found it harder to adjust to life outside of prison when they were released. "The Pell Grant ban [of] 1994 really just decimated college programs in prisons," said Marc Mauer, who directs the Sentencing Project, in 2015. "Today, you can count on two hands the number of colleges or universities

EDUCATION COUNTS

For inmates at the Maryland Correctional Institution for Women, education is a first step in getting their lives back on track. Monnek Hall and Stephanie Spicer, both in their thirties, enrolled in a class called Cultural Psychology: Black Psychology at Goucher College outside Baltimore.

Goucher College is one example of a school that could benefit from the Second Chance Pell Pilot Program. Education Department officials estimate that 100 prisoners will be able to receive grants to obtain bachelor's degrees through Goucher. The college enrolls anywhere from 60 to 100 prisoners at a time. "Access to high-quality education is vital to ensuring that justice-involved individuals have an opportunity to reclaim their lives and restore their futures," said US Attorney General Loretta Lynch in 2016.[13]

Inmates learn computer coding, helping improve their chances of finding a job when they are released from prison.

that are providing any kind of significant programming in prisons around the country."[14]

Once again, the Obama administration took small steps to address these issues. In June 2016, Obama announced the Second Chance Pell Pilot Program, which was intended to address the lack of education opportunities in prisons. According to the plan, the White House intended to release approximately $30 million in Pell Grants to inmates in more than 100 federal and state penitentiaries across 27 states.[15] To lessen the fears of the program's opponents, Obama stated the plan would not affect funding to already eligible Pell recipients who are not incarcerated; it would be designed to help inmates better plan for their reentry into society.

Two former prisoners, both of whom graduated from an education program at San Quentin Prison, got jobs at a company in San Bruno, California.

"We all agree that crime must have consequences, but the men and women who have done their time and paid their debt deserve the opportunity to break with the past and forge new lives in their homes, workplaces, and communities," said Education Secretary John B. King Jr. in 2016. "This belief in second chances is fundamental to who we are as Americans."[16]

Following Trump's victory in the 2016 presidential election, many observers debated whether he would overturn some of Obama's reform measures. In the past, both Trump and Jeff Sessions, Trump's choice for attorney general, questioned the need for programs such as the Second Chance Pell Pilot Program. "Do you think . . . nobody's ever tried a program to reduce recidivism?" Sessions asked during a congressional hearing on sentencing laws in 2015. "My observation over the years of attempts to have education and other kind of character-building programs in prison before they're released doesn't seem to have much benefit."[17]

Despite Sessions's comments, former deputy attorney general Sally Yates was confident the Trump administration would maintain the changes. According to her research, inmates who had access to and participated in correctional education programs had a 43 percent lower chance of returning to prison than those who did not. Fewer returnees to prison would, in turn, save money for the Bureau of Prisons and the tax-paying public. "It's smart from a public safety standpoint, and it's less expensive," Yates said.[18]

| DISCUSSION STARTERS |

- How can obtaining an education while in prison benefit a person upon his or her reentry to society?

- Is it fair for landlords to discriminate against people with criminal records? Why or why not?

- How are felons of color disproportionately affected by losing their right to vote?

CHAPTER EIGHT

THE PRISON REFORM MOVEMENT

In November 2016, Juan Echevarria was fighting an uphill battle. Four years earlier, the 41-year-old Hispanic man had finished a 14-year prison sentence for drug-related manslaughter. He was now working to earn a bachelor's degree from the City University of New York's John Jay College of Criminal Justice. But after five years of school, the first of which was spent in prison, Echevarria was still a sophomore and had $18,000 in student loan debt. He struggled through remedial algebra four times before finally passing the class. Maintaining a good grade point average was a constant source of stress.

In addition to his concerns about school, Echevarria faced a number of other life challenges, such as finding an apartment with a landlord who would rent to convicted felons. Since his release from prison in 2012, he had lived in seven different places, mostly with family members or friends. But none of these living arrangements lasted for long.

Echevarria did not give up. He found a day job working as a case manager at the Center for Alternative Sentencing and Employment Services, a nonprofit organization that assists mentally ill prisoners in reentering society. He also became more active in the Prison-to-College Pipeline, a program administered by the Prisoner Reentry Institute, which helps incarcerated and formerly incarcerated men and women in New York City pursue college degrees. Pipeline enrollees start their first year of school while in prison. Once out, they are funneled through John Jay's College Initiative program. This program provides them with advice on financial aid, which classes to take, and how to survive school while holding down a job.

A 2013 report by the Rand Corporation found that participation in a prisoner education program reduced

An inmate takes a carpentry class at Handlon Correctional Facility in Michigan.

an ex-convict's odds of recidivism by 43 percent. Merely spending time with other students in a similar situation "checks all the boxes" for forming new healthy habits, according to Ruth Delaney of the Vera Institute of Justice, which oversees its own prison-to-college initiative in three states.[1] It seemed to work for Echevarria: at the end of 2016, he was still making progress toward his degree.

ORGANIZATIONS FOR REFORM

The Prison-to-College Pipeline is one of a growing number of programs and organizations working to improve harsh sentencing and prison conditions. Such programs also focus on providing reentry

AN ADVISORY ROLE

In 2008, the Sentencing Project published a manual for policymakers entitled *Reducing Racial Disparity in the Criminal Justice System*. The manual discussed ways to identify the causes of racial biases. It also introduced strategies on how to prevent what it called pervasive problems in law enforcement; pretrial, prosecution, and sentencing practices; prison conditions; and parole and reentry outcomes. Some of its suggestions included developing respectful policing practices and challenging cases of racial profiling. It also suggested protesting disproportionate representation in jury pools and launching public education initiatives on the topic of race relations. In addition, the manual called for examining the role of race in death-penalty cases to determine whether an attorney is sufficiently skilled to represent the client's best interests.

Congressional representatives meet with inmates to discuss a program that would enable prisoners to take college classes.

pathways for US prisoners. Whether it's through research, reporting, or grassroots campaigns led by activists and social workers, people across the United States are increasing their efforts to reduce mass incarceration and racial discrimination in the criminal justice system.

The Anti-Recidivism Coalition (ARC) in California hosts the Ride Home Program, which provides transportation from prison on the day of an inmate's release. ARC's drivers, who are former felons, spend the day with newly released prisoners and help them adjust to new surroundings. They buy them a meal, a bar of soap, and a change of clothes. They also advise them on finding work and help them get in touch with relatives or friends. It's mostly about helping them feel normal again.

The Prison Policy Initiative, founded in 2001, conducts sweeping studies on topics related to prison. Some of the group's papers include *The Racial Geography of Mass Incarceration* (July 2015), *Detaining the Poor: How Money Bail Perpetuates an Endless Cycle of Poverty and Jail Time* (May 10, 2016), and *States of Incarceration: The Global Context 2016* (June 16, 2016). These groundbreaking reports provide lawmakers, members of the media, and activists with powerful, up-to-the-minute data they can then use to advocate for reform.

Groups such as the Innocence Project and

A LIST WORTH KEEPING

Finding a lawyer who will work for free can be a daunting task for a prisoner seeking representation. But Prison Policy Initiative created the first online list of legal services for incarcerated people. The database includes addresses, phone numbers, and background information on law firms and organizations that provide free legal assistance to inmates incarcerated for civil offenses. Each group on the list is contacted every year to determine whether its services are still available.

Northwestern University's Center on Wrongful Convictions (CWC) work to overturn cases of prisoners charged with crimes they did not commit. The CWC uses DNA samples to scrutinize faulty forensic evidence. They investigate false confessions, coerced witness statements, and cases in which a prisoner didn't receive a fair trial due to an impartial jury or ill-prepared attorney. Since launching in 1999, the CWC now receives more than 3,000 requests for services per year. "Our efforts not only free innocent people, they reveal mistakes and missteps at every juncture of our justice system—

THE INNOCENCE PROJECT

On October 19, 1991, police discovered the body of 77-year-old Louise Talley on the second floor of her home in Philadelphia, Pennsylvania. She had been raped and stabbed to death.

The next day, 20-year-old African American Anthony Wright was arrested for the crime. Detectives said he signed a statement confessing his guilt. On June 8, 1993, a jury convicted him of capital murder, rape, theft, burglary, robbery, and weapons violations. He was sentenced to life in prison without the possibility of parole.

Wright served 25 years in prison. But throughout that time, he insisted he wasn't guilty. Wright contacted the Innocence Project, an advocacy group working to overturn wrongful convictions.

On August 23, 2016, a new jury acquitted Wright, and he was released. "DNA testing proved not only that Mr. Wright is absolutely innocent but also that law enforcement fabricated evidence against him," said Peter Neufeld, codirector of the Innocence Project.[2]

from the moment the yellow crime tape goes up until the last appeal," said CWC executive director emeritus Rob Warden.[3]

A LOOK TOWARD THE FUTURE

In the first two decades of the 2000s, race still plays a defining role in every aspect of the criminal justice system. According to some groups, including the Leadership Conference on Civil and Human Rights, instances of racial inequalities are growing, not decreasing. In 1964, Congress passed the Civil Rights Act, which prohibited discrimination in employment. Yet today, three out of every ten African American males born in the United States will spend time in prison.[4] Upon their release, they are likely to be denied employment because of a question about incarceration history on job applications.

In 1965, Congress passed the Voting Rights Act. Yet today, 2.2 million African Americans have lost the right to vote under these laws. Given present rates of incarceration, as many as 40 percent of black men may permanently lose their right to vote in states that disenfranchise ex-offenders.[5]

In 1965, Congress also passed the Immigration and Nationality Act, which attempted to eliminate racial

Inmates attend a graduation ceremony as they complete their high school degrees in prison.

In 2016, California voters approved a measure allowing many nonviolent criminals to be released on parole instead of spending decades in prison.

discrimination in US immigration laws. But according to the Leadership Conference, discrimination is still a major problem today. Racial and ethnic minorities are routinely singled out for immigration enforcement, detained at airports and borders, and put into detention centers for indeterminate periods away from their families.

Juan Echevarria, Carlos Cervantes, and other former prisoners are forging new roads to rehabilitation. And prisoner advocacy groups across the United States are pushing lawmakers and White House administrators to enact measures that might curb racial disparity. "We could choose to be a nation that extends care, compassion, and concern to those who are locked up and locked out or headed for prison before they are old enough to vote," said author Michelle Alexander. "If we want to do more than just end mass incarceration—if we want to put an end to the history of racial caste in America—we must lay down our racial bribes, join hands with people of all colors who are not content to wait for change to trickle down, and say to those who would stand in our way: Accept all of us or none."[6]

DISCUSSION STARTERS

- Do you think racial discrimination exists in the criminal justice system? Why or why not?

- How might the US government work to improve the way it treats people of color in the criminal justice system?

- What do you think about Michelle Alexander's quote in the last paragraph? Do you think such a thing is possible?

- Would you want to volunteer to help inspire change in the criminal justice system? What steps do you think would be the most effective?

ESSENTIAL FACTS

SIGNIFICANT EVENTS

- Enacted in 1968, the Fair Housing Act shielded renters from discrimination by landlords. It included a clause denying criminals these protections.

- The 1986 Anti-Drug Abuse Act established a mandatory five-year minimum sentence for possession of five grams of crack, a cheap and smokable form of cocaine. Those caught with the powdered form of the drug—mostly wealthy white drug users—had to be caught with 500 grams to receive the mandatory minimum sentence.

- The 1994 Violent Crime Control and Law Enforcement Act barred inmates in federal and state prisons from having access to Pell Grants.

KEY PLAYERS

- Founded in 1989, Equal Justice Initiative is a nonprofit organization that provides legal representation to people who have been illegally convicted, wrongly sentenced, or treated poorly in state jails and prisons.

- Prison Policy Initiative is a nonprofit, nonpartisan organization founded in 2001 to address misconduct in the US prison system. Through research and advocacy campaigns, it aims to provide the public with information about injustices in incarceration practices.

- The Sentencing Project is dedicated to reforming sentencing practices in the US criminal justice system. Founded in 1986, the nonprofit organization fights against unjust racial disparities and practices, and it promotes alternatives to incarceration.

IMPACT ON SOCIETY

Under the Thirteenth Amendment to the US Constitution, which was ratified in 1865, four million African Americans were freed from slavery. However, convicts were denied rights under the amendment. Consequently, some historians believe this unleashed a decades-long trend toward enslaving blacks and other minorities in a different way: by making them criminals and, therefore, exempt from protection. Through methods such as the convict leasing system and chain gangs in the early 1900s, the Jim Crow laws of the late 1800s to the mid-1900s, the mass incarceration of minorities in the war on drugs of the 1970s, 1980s, and 1990s, and the way immigrants are detained and deported today, people of color face significant discrimination in the criminal justice system. Through education reform and reentry programs, much work is being done to bring about change.

QUOTE

"We are a nation that professes freedom yet have this mass incarceration, this hyper-incarceration system . . . that is grinding into it our most vulnerable citizenry—and is overwhelmingly biased towards people of color."

—*US Senator Cory Booker*

GLOSSARY

ASYLUM

Protection given by a country to someone who has left his or her country as a political refugee.

BIAS

Prejudice in favor of or against one thing, person, or group compared with another, usually in a way considered to be unfair.

COMMUTE

To downgrade or change to a lesser sentence, usually in prison terms.

DEPORTATION

The expulsion of a person from a country through a legal process.

DISCRIMINATE

To judge a person positively or negatively on the basis of race, class, sex, or other category.

DISPARITY

A great difference.

DUE PROCESS

In legal matters, when no citizen may be denied his or her legal rights.

INCARCERATION

The act of putting someone in prison or jail.

LYNCHING

The act of illegally killing a person through mob action.

PAROLE

The release of a prisoner prior to the end of the maximum sentence imposed.

PREJUDICIAL

Causing biased or pointed opinions about a certain race, sex, gender, or other group; discriminatory.

RACIAL PROFILING

Using racial characteristics to determine whether a person may be committing an illegal activity.

RECIDIVISM

Falling again into crime; returning to prison.

SEGREGATION

The practice of separating groups of people based on race, gender, ethnicity, or other factors.

SLANDER

A false statement that harms someone's reputation.

ADDITIONAL RESOURCES

SELECTED BIBLIOGRAPHY

Alexander, Michelle. *The New Jim Crow: Mass Incarceration in the Age of Colorblindness*. New York: New, 2012. Print.

Mauer, Marc. "Addressing Racial Disparities in Incarceration." *The Prison Journal*. The Sentencing Project, 2011. Print.

"Racial Justice." *EJI*. Equal Justice Initiative, 2016. Web. 3 Nov. 2016.

FURTHER READINGS

Buckley, A.M. *Racism*. Minneapolis: Abdo, 2011. Print.

Kanefield, Teri. *Guilty?: Crime, Punishment, and the Changing Face of Criminal Justice*. Boston: Houghton, 2014. Print.

Vander Hook, Sue. *Miranda v. Arizona: An Individual's Rights When under Arrest*. Minneapolis: Abdo, 2013. Print.

WEBSITES

To learn more about Race in America, visit **abdobooklinks.com**. These links are routinely monitored and updated to provide the most current information available.

FOR MORE INFORMATION

For more information on this subject, contact or visit the following organizations:

ALCATRAZ ISLAND
B201 Fort Mason
Golden Gate National Recreation Area
San Francisco, CA 94122
415-561-4900
https://www.nps.gov/alca/index.htm

Through hands-on visual and audio exhibits, learn about what incarceration was like when the jail was still running and feel what it's like to be locked inside a jail cell. A tour of the grounds promises stunning views of San Francisco Bay.

FROM ENSLAVEMENT TO MASS INCARCERATION MUSEUM
122 Commerce Street
Montgomery, AL 36104
334-269-1803
http://eji.org/enslavement-to-mass-incarceration-museum

Sponsored by the Equal Justice Initiative, this museum is the first of its kind in the nation and features interactive displays about the history of racial inequality in the United States. Exhibits include photographs, informative displays, and virtual reality films about the domestic slave trade, lynching, segregation, police violence, and mass incarceration.

NATIONAL MUSEUM OF AFRICAN AMERICAN HISTORY & CULTURE
1400 Constitution Avenue NW
Washington, DC 20560
844-750-3012
https://nmaahc.si.edu/

Part of the Smithsonian Institution, the National Museum of African American History and Culture is the only national museum devoted solely to the documentation of African American life, history, and culture.

SOURCE NOTES

CHAPTER 1. THE DEATH OF SANDRA BLAND

1. Bryan Smith. "An American Tragedy." *Chicago*. Chicago Tribune Media Group, 14 Dec. 2015. Web. 18 Nov. 2016.
2. Ibid.
3. "Trooper in Sandra Bland Traffic Stop Formally Fired." *NBC News*. NBC News, 2 Mar. 2016. Web. 18 Nov. 2016.
4. Bryan Smith. "An American Tragedy." *Chicago*. Chicago Tribune Media Group, 14 Dec. 2015. Web. 18 Nov. 2016.
5. Neena Satija and Nicole Cobler. "In County Where Sandra Bland Died, Sheriff Is Re-elected." *Texas Tribune*. Texas Tribune, 9 Nov. 2016. Web. 18 Nov. 2016.
6. Dana Liebelson and Ryan J. Reilly. "Sandra Bland Died One Year Ago and Since Then, At Least 810 People Have Lost Their Lives in Jail." *Huffington Post*. TheHuffingtonPost.com Inc., 13 July 2016. Web. 18 Nov. 2016.
7. Margaret Noonan, Harley Rohloff, and Scott Ginder. "Mortality in Local Jails and State Prisons, 2000–2013 – Statistical Tables." *Bureau of Justice Statistics*. US Department of Justice, Aug. 2015. Web. 1 Mar. 2017.
8. Gabrielle Banks. "Sandra Bland Wrongful Death Case Resolved." *Houston Chronicle*. Hearst Newspapers, 2 Nov. 2016. Web. 18 Nov. 2016.

CHAPTER 2. A NEW CENTURY DIVIDED

1. "Issues: Racial Disparity." *Sentencing Project*. Sentencing Project, n.d. Web. 2 Nov. 2016.
2. "Primary Documents in American History: 13th Amendment to the US Constitution." *Library of Congress*. Library of Congress, 30 Nov. 2015. Web. 2 Nov. 2016.
3. "Slavery by Another Name: Convict Leasing." *PBS*. PBS, n.d. Web. 2 Nov. 2016.
4. Ibid.
5. "History of Lynchings." *NAACP*. NAACP, n.d. Web. 2 Nov. 2016.
6. "Trail of Tears." *History*. A&E Television Networks, 2009. Web. 2 Nov. 2016.
7. "America in the Second World War: Japanese-American Internment." *USHistory*. Independence Hall Association, n.d. Web. 2 Nov. 2016.
8. "Internment History." *PBS*. PBS, n.d. Web. 2 Nov. 2016.
9. Julie Turkewitz. "Revisiting a World War II Internment Camp, as Others Try to Keep Its Story from Fading." *New York Times*. New York Times, 17 May 2015. Web. 2 Nov. 2016.
10. *13th*. Dir. Ava DuVernay. Kandoo Films/Netflix, 2016. Film.

CHAPTER 3. THE WAR ON DRUGS

1. "Trends in US Corrections." *Sentencing Project*. Sentencing Project, Dec. 2015. Web. 1 Mar. 2017.
2. "The Drug War, Mass Incarceration and Race." *Drug Policy Alliance*. Drug Policy Alliance, Feb. 2016. Web. 12 Jan. 2017.
3. "World Report 2016: United States." *Human Rights Watch*. Human Rights Watch, n.d. Web. 1 Mar. 2017.
4. "The Drug War, Mass Incarceration and Race." *Drug Policy Alliance*. Drug Policy Alliance, Feb. 2016. Web. 12 Jan. 2017.
5. *13th*. Dir. Ava DuVernay. Kandoo Films/Netflix, 2016. Film.

6. Jennifer Robison. "Decades of Drug Use: The '80s and '90s." *Gallup*. Gallup, 9 July 2002. Web. 2 Mar. 2017.

7. "Drugs and Crime Facts, 1989." *US Department of Justice*. US Department of Justice, Jan. 1990. Web. 2 Mar. 2017.

8. *13th*. Dir. Ava DuVernay. Kandoo Films/Netflix, 2016. Film.

9. Ibid.

10. "A Brief History of the Drug War." *Drug Policy Alliance*. Drug Policy Alliance, n.d. Web. 1 Mar. 2017.

11. *13th*. Dir. Ava DuVernay. Kandoo Films/Netflix, 2016. Film.

12. "The Drug War, Mass Incarceration and Race." *Drug Policy Alliance*. Drug Policy Alliance, Feb. 2016. Web. 12 Jan. 2017.

13. Michael D. Shear. "Obama Commutes Sentences for 61 Convicted of Drug Crimes." *New York Times*. New York Times, 30 Mar. 2016. Web. 1 Mar. 2017.

14. Gregory Korte. "Obama Grants 78 Pre-Christmas Pardons in Last-Minute Clemency Push." *USA Today*. USA Today, 19 Dec. 2016. Web. 12 Jan. 2017.

15. Kevin Freking. "111 Will Be Freed under Obama's Latest Commutation of Nonviolent Drug Offenders." *PBS*. PBS, 30 Aug. 2016. Web. 1 Mar. 2017.

16. Peter Wagner and Bernadette Rabuy. "Mass Incarceration: The Whole Pie 2016." *Prison Policy Initiative*. Prison Policy Initiative, 14 Mar. 2016. Web. 1 Mar. 2017.

17. Charlie Savage. "US to Phase Out Use of Private Prisons for Federal Inmates." *New York Times*. New York Times, 18 Aug. 2016. Web. 1 Mar. 2017.

CHAPTER 4. IMMIGRATION AND THE CRIMINAL JUSTICE SYSTEM

1. Matt Sepic. "Brought as Kids, Possibly Deported as Adults, Several Cambodians Await Federal Action." *MPR News*. Minnesota Public Radio, 15 Sept. 2016. Web. 1 Mar. 2017.

2. "Who We Are." *US Immigrations and Customs Enforcement*. US Immigrations and Customs Enforcement, n.d. Web. 1 Mar. 2017.

3. "FY 2016 ICE Immigration Removals." *US Immigration and Customs Enforcement*. US Immigration and Customs Enforcement, n.d. Web. 1 Mar. 2017.

4. Catherine E. Shoichet. "Immigrants and Crime: Crunching the Numbers." *CNN*. Cable News Network, 8 July 2015. Web. 1 Mar. 2017.

5. "Two Systems of Justice: How the Immigration System Falls Short of American Ideals of Justice." *American Immigration Council*. American Immigration Council, Mar. 2013. Web. 1 Mar. 2017.

6. "US: Deaths in Immigration Detention." *Human Rights Watch*. Human Rights Watch, 7 July 2016. Web. 1 Mar. 2017.

7. Stephen Dinan. "Illegal Immigrant Detention Centers Rife with Abuses, US Civil Rights Commission Report Finds." *Washington Times*. Washington Times, 17 Sept. 2015. Web. 1 Mar. 2017.

8. Marlon Bishop and Fernanda Echávarri. "The Strange Death of José de Jesús." *Marshall Project*. Marshall Project, 22 July 2016. Web. 1 Mar. 2017.

9. "Two Systems of Justice: How the Immigration System Falls Short of American Ideals of Justice." *American Immigration Council*. American Immigration Council, Mar. 2013. Web. 1 Mar. 2017.

CHAPTER 5. THE SCOURGE IN SENTENCING

1. Sarah Childress. "Michelle Alexander: 'A System of Racial and Social Control.'" *Frontline*. WGBH Educational Foundation/PBS, 29 Apr. 2014. Web. 18 Nov. 2016.

2. The Prisons Bureau. "Annual Determination of Average Cost of Incarceration." *Federal Register*. Federal Register, 9 Mar. 2015. Web. 18 Nov. 2016.

3. Jennifer Turner and Jamil Dakwar. "Written Submission of the American Civil Liberties Union on Racial Disparities in Sentencing." *American Civil Liberties Union*. American Civil Liberties Union, 27 Oct. 2014. Web. 18 Nov. 2016.

SOURCE
NOTES CONTINUED

4. Andrew Kahn and Chris Kirk. "What It's Like to Be Black in the Criminal Justice System." *Slate*. Slate, 9 Aug. 2015. Web. 1 Mar. 2017.

5. "Excessive Sentences for Drug and Property Crimes; Extreme Racial Disparities Shown." *American Civil Liberties Union*. American Civil Liberties Union, 13 Nov. 2013. Web. 18 Nov. 2016.

6. Ibid.

7. Gene Demby. "Study Reveals Worse Outcomes for Black and Latino Defendants." *Code Switch*. NPR, 17 July 2014. Web. 18 Nov. 2016.

8. Ariane de Vogue. "Supreme Court Sides with Death Row Inmate in Racial Discrimination Case." *CNN*. Cable News Network, 23 May 2016. Web. 18 Nov. 2016.

9. Nina Totenberg. "US Supreme Court Decides 3 Cases Involving Race." *The Two-Way*. NPR, 23 May 2016. Web. 18 Nov. 2016.

10. Nicholas Fandos. "A Study Documents the Paucity of Black Elected Prosecutors: Zero in Most States." *New York Times*. New York Times, 7 July 2015. Web. 18 Nov. 2016.

11. Ibid.

12. Ibid.

CHAPTER 6. BEHIND BARS

1. "What We Know about Violence in America's Prisons." *Mother Jones*. Mother Jones and the Foundation for National Progress, July/Aug. 2016. Web. 1 Mar. 2017.

2. Jamal Hagler. "8 Facts You Should Know about the Criminal Justice System and People of Color." *Center for American Progress*. Center for American Progress, 28 May 2015. Web. 1 Mar. 2017.

3. "Criminal Justice Facts." *Sentencing Project*. Sentencing Project, n.d. Web. 1 Mar. 2017.

4. Margaret Noonan, Harley Rohloff, and Scott Ginder. "Mortality in Local Jails and State Prisons, 2000–2013 – Statistical Tables." *Bureau of Justice Statistics*. US Department of Justice, Aug. 2015. Web. 1 Mar. 2017.

5. Rachel Gandy. "In Prisons, Blacks and Latinos Do the Time while Whites Get the Jobs." *Prison Policy Initiative*. Prison Policy Initiative, 10 July 2015. Web. 1 Mar. 2017.

6. "Incarcerated Women and Girls." *Sentencing Project*. Sentencing Project, Nov. 2015. Web. 1 Mar. 2017.

7. Kim Severson. "Troubles at Women's Prison Test Alabama." *New York Times*. New York Times, 1 Mar. 2014. Web. 1 Mar. 2017.

8. Jamal Hagler. "8 Facts You Should Know about the Criminal Justice System and People of Color." *Center for American Progress*. Center for American Progress, 28 May 2015. Web. 1 Mar. 2017.

9. Timothy Williams. "Number of Women in Jail Has Grown Far Faster Than That of Men, Study Says." *New York Times*. New York Times, 17 Aug. 2016. Web. 1 Mar. 2017.

10. Alex Ronan. "Menstruation Can Become Humiliation in Prisons." *New York Magazine*. New York Media, 16 June 2016. Web. 1 Mar. 2017.

11. Alexa Garcia-Ditta. "Expecting Care." *Texas Observer*. Texas Observer, 19 Aug. 2015. Web. 1 Mar. 2017.

CHAPTER 7. POST-PRISON PREJUDICE

1. Loretta Lynch. "Loretta Lynch: Remove Roadblocks Faced by Former Prisoners Re-Entering Society." *USA Today*. USA Today, 27 Apr. 2016. Web. 1 Mar. 2017.

2. Katherine J. Rosich. *Race, Ethnicity, and the Criminal Justice System*. Washington, DC: American Sociological Association, 2007. Print.

3. Sophia Kerby. "The Top 10 Most Startling Facts about People of Color and Criminal Justice in the United States." *Center for American Progress*. Center for American Progress, 13 Mar. 2012. Web. 2 Nov. 2016.

4. Dorsey Nunn and Meredith Desautels. "Ending the Racial Caste System through Reentry Reform." *Huffington Post*. TheHuffingtonPost.com Inc., 29 Sept. 2016. Web. 2 Nov. 2016.

5. Marc Mauer and Virginia McCalmont. "A Lifetime of Punishment: The Impact of the Felony Drug Ban on Welfare Benefits." *Sentencing Project*. Sentencing Project, 14 Nov. 2013. Web. 1 Mar. 2017.

6. Jean Chung. "Felony Disenfranchisement: A Primer." *Sentencing Project*. Sentencing Project, 10 May 2016. Web. 1 Mar. 2017.

7. George Brooks. "Felon Disenfranchisement: Law, History, Policy, and Politics." *Fordham University*. Fordham University, 2004. Web. 2 Mar. 2017.

8. Jean Chung. "Felony Disenfranchisement: A Primer." *Sentencing Project*. Sentencing Project, 10 May 2016. Web. 1 Mar. 2017.

9. Ibid.

10. Sarah Childress. "Michelle Alexander: 'A System of Racial and Social Control.'" *Frontline*. PBS/WGBH Educational Foundation, 29 Apr. 2014. Web. 2 Nov. 2016.

11. Joe Davidson. "'Invisible Punishment' Hits Ex-Felons for Life; DOJ, HUD Fight Blanket Rental Bias." *Washington Post*. Washington Post, 27 Oct. 2016. Web. 2 Nov. 2016.

12. "Office of General Counsel Guidance on Application of Fair Housing Act Standards to the Use of Criminal Records by Providers of Housing and Real Estate-Related Transactions." Washington, DC: US Department of Housing and Urban Development, 4 Apr. 2016. Print.

13. "Why Aren't There More Higher Ed Programs Behind Bars?" *Sentencing Project*. Sentencing Project, 7 Sept. 2015. Web. 2 Nov. 2016.

14. Danielle Douglas-Gabriel. "12,000 Inmates to Receive Pell Grants to Take College Classes." *Washington Post*. Washington Post, 24 June 2016. Web. 2 Nov. 2016.

15. Ibid.

16. Ibid.

17. Matt Zapotosky and Sari Horwitz. "The Justice Department Just Unveiled New Prison Reforms. But the Trump Administration Might Scrap Them." *Washington Post*. Washington Post, 30 Nov. 2016. Web. 1 Mar. 2017.

18. Ibid.

CHAPTER 8. THE PRISON REFORM MOVEMENT

1. Kyle Spencer. "Life Beyond Bars: One Man's Journey from Prison to College." *New York Times*. New York Times, 1 Nov. 2016. Web. 2 Nov. 2016.

2. "With New DNA Testing Proving Innocence, Philly Man Acquitted of Murder in Less Than An Hour after Retrial." *Innocence Project*. Innocence Project, 23 Aug. 2016. Web. 2 Nov. 2016.

3. "About Us." *Center on Wrongful Convictions*. Northwestern University Pritzker School of Law, n.d. Web. 2 Nov. 2016.

4. "Justice on Trial: Racial Disparities in the American Criminal Justice System." *Leadership Conference*. Leadership Conference on Civil and Human Rights, n.d. Web. 1 Mar. 2017.

5. "Felony Disenfranchisement Laws in The United States." *Sentencing Project*. Sentencing Project, 28 Apr. 2014. Web. 2 Nov. 2016.

6. Michelle Alexander. *The New Jim Crow: Mass Incarceration in the Age of Colorblindness*. New York. New, 2012. Print. 258.

INDEX

ABOUT THE AUTHOR

Alexis Burling has written dozens of articles and books for young readers on a variety of topics including current and historical events, biographies of famous people, nutrition and fitness, careers, and money management. She is also a book critic with reviews of both adult and young adult books, author interviews, and other industry-related articles published in the *New York Times*, the *Washington Post*, the *San Francisco Chronicle*, and more.